WISE OWL BOOKS

Ok, let's get started with a few funnies to warm the laughing gear ...

Q: What starts with the letter "t," is filled with "t," and ends in "t"?

A: A teapot!

Q: What can be broken, but can't be held?

A: A promise!

Q: What is the longest word in the dictionary?

A: "Smiles," because there's a "mile"

between each "s!"

Q: How do you know if your clock is crazy?

A: It goes "cuckoo!"

Q: What do you get when you cross a parrot and

a centipede?

A: A walkie-talkie!

Q: Why do birds fly south in the winter?

A: Because it's too far to walk!

Q: Why did the cat run away from the tree

A: Because he was afraid of its bark!

Q: What has a face and two hands, but no arms

or legs?

A: A clock!

Q: When does Friday come before Thursday?

A: In the dictionary!

Ok, now that you've had a few laughs, are you ready for the first word search? The words are from the jokes you've just read. Can you find which jokes they were in?

Word Search

J	L	T	L	B	I	R	D	U	A	G	I
M	W	E	H	Q	R	A	I	N	Z	D	M
S	A	A	F	R	I	D	A	Y	C	C	I
J	L	P	O	S	O	U	T	H	L	A	L
K	K	O	X	W	O	R	D	S	O	R	E
R	T	T	Y	H	W	E	T	E	C	D	M
L	E	A	C	H	B	A	B	D	K	F	I
R	U	N	R	D	U	Q	E	O	M	C	N

Find the following words in the puzzle.

Words are hidden ->, and ↓.

Bird   Mile   Wet

Card   Rain   Word

Clock   South   Friday

Each   Teapot   Walk

TONGUE TWISTERS FOR PRACTICE

Here's some easy tongue twisters to get you started. Practice saying them three times, getting faster each time.

Daddy Draws Doors

She sees cheesy cheese sticks.

Six socks sit in a sink

Six socks sit in a sink, soaking in soap suds

Q: What is green and sings?

A: Elvis Parsley!

Q: What do you call an elephant in a phone booth?

A: Stuck!

Q: What succeeds?

A: A budgie with a broken beak!

Q: Where do you learn to make banana splits?

A: At sundae school!

Q: What never asks questions, but is often

answered?

A: A doorbell!

Q: What comes down, but never comes up?

A: Rain!

Q: Why was the student's report card wet?

A: It was below C level!

Q: Why did the melon jump into the lake?

A: It wanted to be a "water-melon!"

Q: What is the difference between a unicorn and

a carrot?

A: One is a funny beast and the other is a bunny

feast!

Q: What's the problem with twin witches?

A: You can't tell which witch is which!

Q: What do you call a fake noodle?

A: An impasta!

Q: What did the asparagus say to the mushroom?

A: You're a fun guy!

Q: What's the best thing to put into a pie?

A: Your teeth!

Q: What's large, grey and wears glass slippers?

A: Cinderellephant!

Q: How do you catch a monkey?

A: Climb a tree and act like a banana!

Here's another word search you can try. Can you find them in the jokes as well?

Word Search

```
B  B  B  U  N  N  Y  W  E  S  A  S
R  E  A  N  D  K  T  I  L  U  I  C
U  A  N  I  M  A  E  T  E  W  G  H
L  K  A  C  A  K  E  C  P  Z  L  O
Q  C  N  O  Q  C  T  H  H  G  A  O
E  B  A  R  T  F  H  Y  A  W  S  L
N  I  C  N  L  A  K  E  N  C  S  F
F  U  N  (P  H  O  N  E)  T  P  A  Y
```

Find the following words in the puzzle.

Words are hidden ->, and ↓.

(Phone)   School   Witch
Elephant   Lake   Fun
Beak   Unicorn   Teeth
Glass   Bunny   Banana

TONGUE TWISTERS 2

This tongue twister is like a poem, can you work out which horse won?!

One-One was a racehorse.

Two-Two was one, too.

When One-One won one race,

Two-Two won one, too.

Q: What bird is with you at every meal?

A: A swallow!

Q: What do ghosts use to clean their hair?

A: Sham-boo!

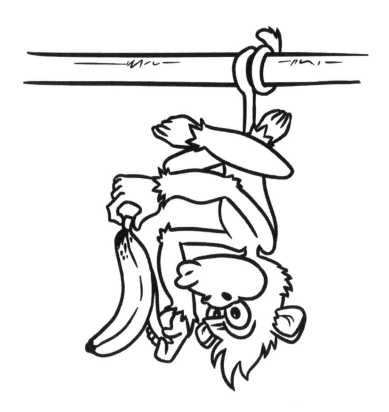

Q: Why do monkeys like to eat bananas?

A: Because they have appeal!

Q: What do you call a shoe made from a banana?

A: A slipper!

Q: Why did the banana go to the doctor?

A: Because it wasn't peeling well!

Q: What do you get when a chicken lays an egg

on top of a barn?

A: An eggroll!

Q: Why did the cabbage win the race?

A: Because it was ahead!

Q: What happens if you eat a dinner of yeast and shoe polish?

A: You'll rise and shine in the morning!

Q: What do you call a cow with two legs?

A: Lean beef!

Q: What do you call a cow with no legs?

A: Ground beef!

Q: What do sea monsters eat for lunch?

A: Fish and ships!

Q: What do ghosts eat on Halloween?

A: Ghoulash!

Q: What cheese is made backwards?

A: Edam!

Q: How do chickens bake a cake?

A: From scratch!

Q: What room is useless for a ghost?

A: A living room!

Q: Why did Eeyore look in the loo?

A: Because he was looking for Pooh!

Q: What do you call a bear with no teeth?

A: A gummy bear!

Q: What did the baby corn say to the mama corn?

A: Where's pop?

Q: What did the skeleton order for dinner?

A: Spare ribs!

Q: What did the nut say when it sneezed?

A: Cashew!

_____

Ready for the next word search?

Word Search

```
Y  T  B  C  D  M  O  N  K  E  Y  D
M  F  O  C  I  O  E  R  Z  P  P  O
H  I  S  O  N  Z  Y  C  B  I  M  C
E  S  H  W  N  P  B  O  E  C  Y  T
N  H  O  E  E  G  P  R  E  K  H  O
Z  A  E  Y  R  R  X  N  F  L  E  R
L  E  G  G  S  R  K  G  H  E  X  S
N  G  H  O  S  T  F  H  B  Z  D  J
```

Find the following words in the puzzle.

Words are hidden ->, and ↓.

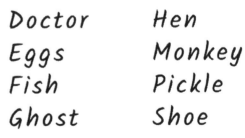

Doctor   Hen
Eggs   Monkey
Fish   Pickle
Ghost   Shoe

Beef
Corn
Cow
Dinner

24

TONGUE TWISTERS 3

Starting to get a little harder now. See how fast you can go!!!

Nine nimble noblemen nibbling nine nuts each.

At a minute or two to two today

A proper copper coffee pot.

Each Easter Eddie eats eighty Easter eggs.

Q: What does an evil hen lay?

A: Deviled eggs!

Q: What road has the most ghosts haunting it?

A: A dead end!

Q: What does a mixed-up hen lay?

A: Scrambled eggs!

Q: Why was the cucumber mad?

A: Because it was in a pickle!

Q: What do you call an alligator with a magnifying glass?

A: An investi-gator!

Q: What do you call cheese that's not your cheese?

A: Nacho cheese!

Q: What do you get if you cross a fish and an elephant?

A: Swimming trunks!

Q: What do you get when you cross a Labrador and a magician?

A: A labracadabrador!

Q: Where do bees go to the bathroom?

A: The BP station!

Q: What do you call a sleeping bull?

A: A bulldozer!

Q: Why do sharks swim in saltwater?

A: Because pepper water makes them sneeze!

Q: What do you call a grizzly bear caught in the rain?

A: A drizzly bear!

Q: What color socks do bears wear?

They don't wear socks, they have bear feet!

Q: Why do hummingbirds hum?

A: Because they forgot the words!

Q: What is a deer with no eyes called?

... No idea (eye-deer)!

Q: What do you get if you pamper a cow?

A: Spoiled milk!

———————————————

Ready for the next word search?

Word Search

```
Z  H  O  S  P  I  T  A  L  W  Y  Z
D  O  G  A  Y  Q  S  O  D  G  L  L
B  S  H  A  R  K  S  L  J  Z  G  L
A  L  L  I  G  A  T  O  R  K  R  Y
A  N  U  T  H  S  S  W  I  M  O  C
C  A  S  H  E  W  M  I  L  K  A  M
E  E  U  B  E  E  M  S  Y  B  D  U
Q  B  U  L  L  C  H  E  E  S  E  K
```

Find the following words in the puzzle.

Words are hidden ->, and ↓.

Alligator   Cheese   Nut
Bee   Dog   Road
Bull   Hospital   Shark
Cashew   Milk   Swim

TONGUE TWISTERS 4

Ok, these ones really are a mouthful! Try saying each one three times as fast as you can. Good luck!!

If a dog chews shoes, whose shoes does he choose?

Clean clams crammed in clean cans

The boot black brought the black boot back.

Many mumbling mice are making merry music in

the moonlight.

Q: What did Dracula say about his girlfriend?

A: It was love at first bite!

Q: Did you hear the joke about the broken egg?

A: Yes, it cracked me up!

Q: What bird is with you at every meal?

A: A swallow!

Q: What did the mayonnaise say when someone opened the refrigerator door?

A: Close the door, I'm dressing!

Q: Why do seagulls fly over the sea?

A: Because if they flew over the bay, they would be called bagels!

Q: Why did the baker stop making doughnuts?

A: She was bored with the hole business!

Q: Why did the Cyclops stop teaching?

A: Because he only had one pupil!

Q: Why couldn't the teddy bear eat his lunch?

A: Because he was stuffed!

Q: Where do tough chickens come from?

A: Hard-boiled eggs!

Q: What did the angry customer at the Italian restaurant give the chef?

A: A pizza of his mind!

Q: What did the burger name her daughter?

A: Patty!

CUSTOMER: Do you have spaghetti on the menu today?

WAITER: No, I cleaned it off!

Q: How do you fix a broken tomato?

A: With tomato paste!

Q: Why did the pig become an actor?

A: Because he was a ham!

Q: Why do dinosaurs eat raw meat?

A: Because they don't know how to cook!

Q: What do you get from a pampered cow?

A: Spoiled milk!

Q: How do you make a dinosaur float?

A: Put a scoop of ice cream in a glass of root beer

and add one dinosaur!

Q: Which is the left side of a pie?

A: The side that is not eaten!

Q: What weighs 800 pounds and sticks to the roof of your mouth?

A: A peanut butter and Stegosaurus sandwich!

Q: Why did the bird go to hospital?

A: To get tweetment!

Ready for the next word search?

Word Search

```
X  J  J  T  T  L  C  X  L  I  U  I
D  R  E  S  S  V  H  J  U  S  J  C
B  V  M  P  U  T  I  O  N  M  E  E
I  B  S  I  K  M  C  K  C  E  N  C
T  B  A  Z  N  E  K  E  H  A  U  R
E  F  D  Z  Q  A  E  J  D  T  S  E
H  F  R  A  X  L  N  G  P  L  J  A
S  E  A  Y  I  N  W  H  O  L  E  M
```

Find the following words in the puzzle.

Words are hidden ->, and ↓.

Bite	Joke	Pizza
Chicken	Lunch	Ice Cream
Dress	Meal	Sea
Hole	Meat	Sad

TONGUE TWISTERS 5

Ok, here they are, the hardest of the lot. Which one do you think is the hardest. Say them each as fast as you can five times, if you dare!

Eve eating eagerly elegant Easter eggs.

Crisp crusts crackle and crunch.

Growing grey goats graze great green grassy groves.

Fred fed Ted bread and Ted fed Fred bread

Q: Why did the apple go out with a fig?

A: It couldn't find a date!

Q: What do little monsters eat?

A: Alpha-bat soup!

Q: What should you take on a trip to the desert?

A: A thirst-aid kit!

Patient: Doctor, I think I need glasses!

Waiter: You certainly do; this is a restaurant!

Q: What do polar bears eat for lunch?

A: Iceberg-ers!

Q: What's the best thing to put in a pie?

A: Your teeth!

Q: Waiter, will my pizza be long?

A: No sir, it will be round!

Q: Why are graveyards noisy?

A: Because of all the coffin!

Q: What kind of vegetable would you like tonight?

A: Beets me!

Q: What happened to the cannibal who was late to dinner?

A: They gave her the cold shoulder!

Q: What is it called when a cat wins a dog show?

A: A cat-has-trophy!

The next word search has a couple of more words.

Word Search

T	U	G	W	R	O	U	N	D	R	W	P
K	I	T	E	M	O	N	S	T	E	R	X
A	D	E	S	E	R	T	B	E	A	R	K
G	L	A	S	S	J	F	I	G	E	C	C
N	O	I	S	Y	N	L	O	N	G	F	O
P	H	C	V	I	D	A	T	E	H	C	L
D	T	R	A	I	N	S	U	A	A	Q	D
T	V	I	C	A	T	E	Z	D	O	G	G

Find the following words in the puzzle.

Words are hidden ->, and ↓.

Bear	Dog	Monster
Cat	Fig	Noisy
Cold	Glass	Round
Date	Kite	Train
Desert	Long	

Knock, knock.

Who's there?

Lena

Lena who?

Lena little closer and I'll tell you!

Knock, knock.

Who's there?

Justin.

Justin who?

Justin the neighbourhood and thought I'd come

over.

Knock, knock.

Who's there?

Ken

Ken who?

Ken I come in, it's freezing out here?

Knock, knock.

Who's there?

Tyrone

Tyrone who?

Tyrone shoelaces!

Knock, knock.

Who's there?

Nana.

Nana who?

Nana your business who's there.

Knock, knock.

Who's there?

Nobel

Nobel who?

No bell, that's why I knocked!

Knock, knock.

Who's there?

Sherlock.

Sherlock who?

You Sherlock your door up tight!

Knock, knock.

Who's there?

Cash.

Cash who?

No thanks, but I'll take a peanut if you have

one!

Knock, knock.

Who's there?

Cargo!

Cargo who?

Car go beep, beep!

Knock, knock.

Who's there?

Canoe!

Canoe who?

Canoe come out and play with me today?

———————————

Last word search. Are you ready?

Word Search

```
J  X  O  F  B  L  E  S  S  P  P  D
U  S  W  R  C  P  B  U  B  A  P  H
I  K  L  E  L  H  E  I  E  C  H  D
C  N  Z  E  A  E  E  T  L  K  O  E
E  O  D  Z  C  R  P  C  L  M  N  A
F  C  T  I  E  E  G  A  A  R  E  R
N  K  P  N  S  C  H  S  E  E  Y  G
P  E  E  G  N  F  E  E  D  Y  F  Z
```

Find the following words in the puzzle.
Words are hidden ->, and ↓.

Beep	Here	Owl
Bell	Honey	Pack
Bless	Juice	See
Dear	Knock	Suitcase
Freezing	Laces	

Knock, knock.

Who's there?

Wendy.

Wendy who?

Wendy bell works again I won't have to knock

anymore.

Knock, knock.

Who's there?

Will

Will who?

Will you let me in? It's freezing out here!

Knock, knock.

Who's there?

Alpaca

Alpaca who?

Alpaca the trunk, you pack the suitcase!

Knock, knock.

Who's there?

Honey bee.

Honey bee who?

Honey bee a dear and get me some juice.

Knock, knock.

Who's there?

Who

Who who?

Is there an owl in here?

Knock, knock.

Who's there?

Atch!

Atch who?

Bless you!

Knock, knock.

Who's there?

Kent!

Kent who?

Kent you tell who I am by my voice?

Knock, knock.

Who's there?

Amish!

Amish who?

Awe, I miss you too.

Printed in Great Britain
by Amazon